-BEARS OF THE WORLD-

BROWN BEARS

LEE FITZGERALD

PowerKiDS
press

New York

Published in 2017 by The Rosen Publishing Group, Inc.
29 East 21st Street, New York, NY 10010

First Edition

Editor: Katie Kawa
Book Design: Reann Nye

Photo Credits: Cover, pp. 1, 12 Erik Mandre/Shutterstock.com; cover, pp. 1, 3–24 (background) eva_mask/Shutterstock.com; p. 4 Tao Jiang/Shutterstock.com; p. 5 Nagel Photography/Shutterstock.com; p. 6 Canon Boy/Shutterstock.com; p. 7 Radu Bercan/Shutterstock.com; pp. 8, 22 Dennis W. Donohue/Shutterstock.com; p. 9 zizar/Shutterstock.com; p. 10 Galyna Andrushko/Shutterstock.com; p. 11 Meoita/Shutterstock.com; p. 13 Tony Campbell/Shutterstock.com; p. 14 AndreAnita/Shutterstock.com; p. 15 Gleb Tarro/Shutterstoock.com; p. 16 David Rasmus/Shutterstock.com; p. 17 volkova natalia/Shutterstock.com; p. 18 Holly Kuchera/Shutterstock.com; p. 19 ArCaLu/Shutterstock.com; p. 20 Eric Isselee/Shutterstock.com; p. 21 Barrett Hedges/National Geographic/Getty Images.

Cataloging-in-Publication Data

Names: Fitzgerald, Lee.
Title: Brown bears / Lee Fitzgerald.
Description: New York : PowerKids Press, 2017. | Series: Bears of the world | Includes index.
Identifiers: ISBN 9781499420364 (pbk.) | ISBN 9781499420388 (library bound) | ISBN 9781499420371 (6 pack)
Subjects: LCSH: Brown bear-Juvenile literature.
Classification: LCC QL737.C27 F58 2017 | DDC 599.784-d23

Manufactured in the United States of America

CPSIA Compliance Information: Batch #BS16PK: For Further Information contact Rosen Publishing, New York, New York at 1-800-237-9932

CONTENTS

FOUND AROUND THE WORLD

Have you ever seen a grizzly bear? Maybe you've heard of the giant Kodiak bears that live on islands in Alaska. These bears might have different names, but they both belong to the same group of bears called brown bears.

Brown bears are a species, or kind, of bear that lives in many places on Earth. In fact, brown bears live in more parts of the world than any other kind of bear. Do brown bears live in the wild near you? Keep reading to find out!

—Bear Basics—

Grizzly bears are brown bears with fur that sometimes has silver or white tips. "Grizzled" means **streaked** with gray, and that's where the name "grizzly" comes from.

The grizzly bear, shown here, is just one of many kinds of brown bears found around the world.

HOME ON THE RANGE

In North America, brown bears live mainly in Alaska and Canada. A small number of brown bears live in parts of the northwestern **continental** United States. Brown bears are also found in small areas throughout Europe. In Asia, brown bears live in northern parts of the **continent**, as well as the Middle East.

One reason brown bears are found in so many places is because they can live in many different **habitats**. They make their homes in the mountains, forests, and open spaces such as **prairies**.

WHERE BROWN BEARS LIVE

North America

Europe

Asia

brown bears

This map shows the places where brown bears still live in the wild, which is called their range. Brown bears used to live over an even larger area of the planet, but hunting and habitat loss made their range shrink.

BIG BEARS!

Brown bears aren't just big bears—they're huge! Grizzly bears, which are some of the largest brown bears, can weigh more than 800 pounds (363 kg). These bears can also stand more than 8 feet (2.4 m) tall if they rise up on their back legs. Male brown bears are larger than females.

Not all brown bears have the same color fur. It can be as light as cream or so dark it almost looks black. Brown bears are also known for having a hump on their back between their shoulders.

—Bear Basics—

A brown bear's shoulder hump is made of **muscle**. This hump gives a brown bear more strength when it uses its front legs.

Male Kodiak bears, such as the one shown here, are generally considered the largest kind of brown bear on Earth. They can weigh up to 1,720 pounds (780 kg)!

DIGGING A DEN

Brown bears use the strength their shoulder hump gives them to dig dens in the sides of hills. A den is where a brown bear lives in winter. When the weather gets colder and it becomes harder to find food, brown bears go into a kind of deep sleep called torpor. However, they can still be woken up if necessary.

How can brown bears stay asleep for the whole winter? They store up fat in their body during late summer and fall. They live off this extra fat during winter.

—Bear Basics—

Brown bears can eat up to 90 pounds (40.8 kg) of food each day in fall as they get ready to sleep all winter!

Brown bears use their long claws to help them dig.

LIFE AS A CUB

Dens aren't just where adult brown bears sleep—they're also where baby brown bears are born. Baby brown bears, which are called cubs, are born in winter. A mother brown bear most often has two cubs at one time. At first, they're blind and have no fur. They begin to grow as they drink milk from their mother.

In spring, the cubs come out of the den with their mother. She teaches them to find food. Male brown bears don't help care for cubs.

Cubs live with their mother for over two years. Mother brown bears will do anything to **protect** their cubs, including attacking people who get too close to them!

WHAT'S FOR DINNER?

Brown bears are omnivores, which means they eat both plants and other animals. In fact, brown bears will eat almost anything! They use their shoulder hump and claws to dig up plant roots. In addition, they eat fruits, berries, and nuts.

Hunting is another important way brown bears get food. They're powerful predators that kill and eat **mammals** such as mice, squirrels, moose, and deer. They eat sheep and other livestock, too, which can make farmers angry. Brown bears also eat carrion, or animals that are already dead.

Some brown bears eat fish. They travel to streams in summer to catch and eat salmon.

ON THE HUNT

Brown bears have a body built for hunting. They use their large size to attack smaller animals. Even though brown bears are heavy, they still move around fairly easily. They can swim, which helps them catch fish. They can also run at speeds of up to 30 miles (48.3 km) per hour.

Brown bears are solitary animals, which means they mainly live and hunt alone. However, some brown bears gather around food **sources**, such as bodies of water with many salmon.

— Bear Basics —

The only brown bears that stay together for long periods of time are mothers and babies.

WHAT MAKES BROWN BEARS GOOD HUNTERS?

large size	speed
sharp claws	ability to swim
great sense of smell	shoulder hump for extra power

These are some of the most important reasons why brown bears are considered **dangerous** predators.

WHAT HUNTS THEM?

Brown bears are feared hunters, but they're not always safe from being hunted. Although adult brown bears generally aren't hunted by wild animals, cubs are still at risk. Mountain lions, wolves, and other bears will sometimes make a meal of a brown bear cub.

The greatest dangers to brown bears, however, are people. These bears were once hunted for their meat, but now they're mainly hunted for sport. Farmers sometimes kill brown bears because they see these bears as a danger to their livestock.

wolf

Brown bears can live between 20 and 30 years in the wild.

PROTECTING PEOPLE AND BEARS

Hunting is one of the reasons why brown bears don't live over as big an area as they once did. Another reason is habitat **destruction**. When people create building projects, they sometimes take over areas where brown bears live.

Many people are afraid of brown bears. These bears sometimes attack people, but brown bear attacks don't happen very often. They mainly occur when a person surprises a brown bear or when a mother bear feels her cubs are in danger. In general, brown bears try to stay away from people.

—Bear Basics—

Grizzly bears once lived throughout large parts of the United States, including the Great Plains. However, there are now only about 1,000 grizzly bears living in the United States south of Canada.

One way people around the world are working to protect brown bears is through the creation of safe places for them to live. In the United States, these safe places include national parks such as Yellowstone National Park.

THE FUTURE OF BROWN BEARS

National parks and other protected lands are important for the future of brown bears around the world. They're great places to see brown bears in their natural habitat. If you go to a national park to see brown bears, remember to keep your **distance**. It's safer for you and the bears!

Brown bears are some of the biggest bears on Earth. They grow from tiny cubs to mighty predators. It's up to us to make sure brown bears continue to live in many parts of the world for many years to come!

GLOSSARY

continent: One of the seven great masses of land on Earth.

continental: Being part of the lower 48 states of the United States.

dangerous: Not safe.

destruction: Causing so much harm to something that it can't be fixed.

distance: The space between two points.

habitat: The natural home for plants, animals, and other living things.

mammal: Any warm-blooded animal whose babies drink milk and whose body is covered with hair or fur.

muscle: A part of the body that produces motion.

prairie: A large, mostly flat area of land in North America that has few trees and is covered in grasses.

protect: To keep safe.

source: A person, place, or thing from which something comes or where it can be found.

streaked: Marked with stripes.

INDEX

WEBSITES

Due to the changing nature of Internet links, PowerKids Press has developed an online list of websites related to the subject of this book. This site is updated regularly. Please use this link to access the list: www.powerkidslinks.com/bworld/brown